100

THINGS
GOD LOVES
ABOUT YOU

SIMPLE REMINDERS FOR
WHEN YOU NEED THEM MOST

To

_____

From

_____

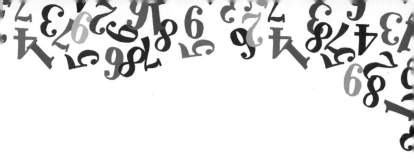

God loves you, and here are some of
the things I love about you too!

_____

_____

_____

_____

ZONDERVAN

100 Things God Loves About You
Copyright © 2014 by Zondervan

Requests for information should be addressed to:

Zondervan, *3900 Sparks Drive., SE, Grand Rapids, MI 49546*

ISBN 978-0-310-34386-8

Cover design: Alexis Ward/The Visual Republic
Cover illustration: Alexis Ward
Interior design: James A. Phinney

Printed in China

19 20 21 22 23 24 25 / DSC / 27 26 25 24 23 22 21 20 19 18 17 16 15 14 13 12 11

100 THINGS
GOD LOVES ABOUT YOU

SIMPLE REMINDERS FOR
WHEN YOU NEED THEM MOST

TAMA FORTNER

1

God loves your story.

*All the days ordained for me
were written in your book
before one of them came to be.*

—PSALM 139:16

You have an amazing story. How can you be sure? Because it was written by Yahweh, the Lord God Himself, before you were even born. He knew every twist of the plot and every unexpected turn. Every joy, every sorrow. Wherever you go, He has already been. He will walk before you and with you as Lord and Guide and Friend. And when you entrust your story to Him, He promises you the best of endings a happily, *heavenly*, forever after.

2

God loves the treasure of you.

Out of all the peoples on the face of the earth, the Lord has chosen you to be his treasured possession.

—DEUTERONOMY 14:2

old and silver? They're just heavenly pavement to Him. Rubies and sapphires? Simple stones for His gates. Diamonds? They're as common as coal. But you? You are His child. You are *precious*. Worth searching for, worth saving, worth every sacrifice. And when God counts up His heavenly treasures, He counts . . . *you*.

3

God loves you, even when you're frazzled and frayed.

"Come to me, all you who are weary and burdened, and I will give you rest."

—MATTHEW 11:28

Already late and that tire couldn't be any flatter. Spaghetti-sauce splatters on your favorite shirt. And that date? Well, yes . . . it was a *definite* disaster! When it feels as if your life is falling apart at the seams, run to God. Rest your world-worn and weary heart in His. When the computer crashes, when your patience is kaput, when it's simply been one of those days, remember that God loves you . . . *even* when you're frazzled and frayed.

4

God loves when you ask Him to forget.

"I, even I, am he who blots out your transgressions, for my own sake, and remembers your sins no more."

—ISAIAH 43:25

God remembers the things you forget. Your wallet, your keys, your best friend's birthday. He remembers everything . . . except what you ask Him to forget. Past mistakes may sometimes haunt you, rising up to point ghostly fingers of blame. But believe in this sweet, beautiful promise: when you ask God to forgive you, He does . . . and then He forgets all about your mistake.

5

God loves to call you His own.

See what great love the Father has lavished on us, that we should be called children of God! And that is what we are!

—1 JOHN 3:1

God loves you. More than just a little. More than a lot. He loves you . . . *lavishly*. His love is not the stingy, strings-attached love of this world. It is a love that stretches beyond the stars and reaches far into eternity. Just call His name, reach out to Him—and His love will sweep into your life, scoop you up, and whisper softly over and over, "You are Mine," . . . for you are His very own.

6

God loves when you let Him carry you.

He gathers the lambs in his arms and carries them close to his heart.

—ISAIAH 40:11

It's hard sometimes, isn't it? The responsibilities, the obligations of daily life. It can sometimes feel as if the weight of the whole world is resting on your shoulders. But the world isn't yours to carry; it's His. When you're too tattered and tired to try yet again, you're too wobbly and weak to keep walking, or you've stumbled down one of life's steep slopes, throw your hands up to Him and say, "I can't do this by myself!" Because when you reach up, He loves to reach down, lift you up, and carry you . . . close to His heart.

7

God loves the beauty of you.

You are altogether beautiful, my darling;
there is no flaw in you.

—SONG OF SONGS 4:7

The world has this definition of what *beauty* is, of what it's supposed to look like. Throw it out. Toss it in the trash heap. Because a true definition of beauty is only found in the One who created it. So open up God's Word and take a look in the mirror of truth. You are a beloved child of the King. You are breathtaking, jaw-dropping, heaven- and heart-stopping. A handcrafted work of art. Don't think you're beautiful? God has something to say about that: my darling, you are *altogether beautiful*!

8

God loves the worth of you.

"Are not five sparrows sold for two pennies? Yet not one of them is forgotten by God. . . . You are worth more than many sparrows."

—LUKE 12:6–7

How much are you worth? The bank has an opinion. So do your teachers and your boss. Even science says that the sum of all your chemical parts is worth only a few dollars. But God says, "You are worth more than many sparrows." Think about that: not a single, tiny sparrow ever falls to the ground unnoticed by God. So imagine how much more He will watch over you! The One who knows the worth of the smallest sparrow also knows and loves the worth of you.

9

God loves all the little things about you.

"The very hairs of your head are all numbered."

—LUKE 12:7

God knows every little thing about you, even the number of hairs on your head. Because He created you. Because He loves you. Yes, every last one of them. That freckle on your cheek? He put it there—in just the right spot. That quirky little giggle? God pitched it and placed it there in your heart. You may look at yourself and see only the flaws, but God doesn't. He loves every little thing about you . . , yes, even that freckle on your cheek.

10

God loves the way you hide in Him.

You are my hiding place;
you will protect me from trouble
and surround me with songs of deliverance.

—PSALM 32:7

When the world comes crashing, banging, stomping, and complaining through your life, it can make you want to turn and run and hide. *So do it!* Run straight to Him. Hide away from the world for a little while. Let God heal your wounded heart. Let Him fill your spirit with His strength and your soul with His songs. Then you can go back and face the world again because God loves the way you hide in Him.

11

God loves living in you.

God is love. Whoever lives in love lives in God, and God in them.

—1 JOHN 4:16

There's no place like home. Not for you. Not for Dorothy. And not for God.

You do realize, don't you, that He could choose anywhere to call home? The grandest palace. The loftiest mountain peak. The highest perch in the heavens. But He didn't choose any of those. He chose a fixer-upper, a work in progress to lovingly restore. He patiently knocked until you answered, and then He moved in. Because the place God most loves to live is . . . in you.

12

God loves the way you love.

Dear friends, let us love one another, for love comes from God. Everyone who loves has been born of God and knows God.

—1 JOHN 4:7

Love. That's really what it's all about, despite what those misguided bumper stickers might say about the hokey-pokey. To be more precise, it's all about *choosing* love because love is a choice. Sometimes it's an easy one. Other times . . . well, it just isn't.

When you choose to walk away instead of striking back, when you choose to honor the parent who isn't so honorable, when you choose to return evil with kindness, God smiles . . . and He loves you for it.

13

God loves your family resemblance.

And we all, who with unveiled faces contemplate the Lord's glory, are being transformed into his image with ever-increasing glory, which comes from the Lord, who is the Spirit.

—2 CORINTHIANS 3:18

Do you giggle like your mom? Or chuckle and chortle like your dad? Do you remind everyone of your Great-Aunt Ruth? We tend to look and act like the people we're related to—those whom we love.

So . . . are you as kind as the King? Do you love like your Lord? Do you give like Jesus? Having your mom's eyes or your dad's smile is great, but when it comes to your heart, God is hoping it looks a lot like His. Because He just loves to see your family resemblance.

14

God loves the way you live like Jesus.

Whoever claims to live in him must live as Jesus did.

—1 JOHN 2:6

Live as Jesus did." Four simple but life-changing words. Because Jesus came to be not only your Savior but also your example.

You live like Jesus when you remember the Samaritan woman and offer the water of life to those others scorn, when you remember Peter and forgive the friend who deserted you, when you remember the woman thrown in the dirt and reach down to lift up one who has fallen.

When you notice the unnoticed, touch the untouchable, love the unloved . . . God loves the way you live like His Son.

15

God loves the way you shine.

You will shine among them like stars in the sky as you hold firmly to the word of life.

—PHILIPPIANS 2:15–16

The world likes to whisper, to tempt, and to taunt. *Just once won't hurt. Go ahead, try it. No one ever has to know.*

But you know the truth, and you choose to stand up for it, for Him. You choose to say evil really is evil and good really is good. You choose to do right when everyone around you chooses wrong. And as proud as any papa, the Lord thumps His chest at the Devil and says, "You see that one? She's mine—just look at her shine!"

16

God loves the way you forgive.

God demonstrates his own love for us in this: While we were still sinners, Christ died for us.

—ROMANS 5:8

Okay, that one hurt, didn't it? Did he really have to say *that*? Did she really just *do* that? To you?

It stings, it hurts, maybe it even scars. But it's time to let it go. Maybe she apologized, and maybe he didn't. But let it go anyway. After all, that's what Jesus did for you—while you were still lost in sin, still hurting Him, He offered to forgive you. And He asks that you do the same. No, it isn't always easy. It will take some time and some prayer. But your forgiving heart is one more thing God loves about you.

17

God loves you even when you are lost.

"For the Son of Man came to seek and to save the lost."

—LUKE 19:10

You wandered away for a moment, for a while, maybe for far too long. But now you're out there, in the wilderness of the world, lost and lonely. Hold on, He's coming.

God is coming. He's left the ninety-nine safe in the fold. Hands stuffed into heavenly pockets, shoulder to the wind, He searches through every sin-soaked, tear-stained corner of the world until He finds you, His treasure, His pearl. He carefully dusts off the grit and grime, brushes away the tears, lifts you into His arms, and begins the journey home—rejoicing because the one who was lost, the one He loves, is now found.

18

God loves you—imperfections and all.

But he said to me, "My grace is sufficient for you, for my power is made perfect in weakness."

—2 CORINTHIANS 12:9

So maybe you can't spell *Wednesday* (*Why is there a "d" in there, anyway?*). Or can't boil water. Or you're late everywhere you go. God still loves you.

Or maybe your struggles go a little deeper than spelling or cooking or clocks. A weakness for gossip? Procrastinating about prayer? A too-short temper with a too-long memory? God still loves you. Why? *Because your imperfections are an invitation for His grace.* They remind you that you need Him. They let Him work in your life, to make you more like Him. Yes, God still loves you . . . imperfections and all.

19

God loves the way you make Him sing.

"The LORD your God is with you,
the Mighty Warrior who saves.
He will take great delight in you;
in his love he will no longer rebuke you,
but will rejoice over you with singing."

—ZEPHANIAH 3:17

Alto, soprano, baritone, and bass—they all blend together to make a joyful noise. But no earthly chorus could ever compare to the heavenly notes of the voice of our Lord and King.

What could make such a Singer sing? Nothing less than the very best of all His creation . . . you. Yes, you! When you live your life—all that you say and do—to the glory of your King, you make God sing!

20

God simply loves to love you.

*"As the Father has loved me,
so have I loved you."*

—JOHN 15:9

Ever dream about that guy? You know, *that* guy. The one who's crazy about you, who can't wait to spend time with you. The one so in love with you that he constantly sends you little gifts to let you know he's thinking about you.

Well, *that* guy is real. No, really! No matter what your relationship status might be, *that* Guy is crazy about you, can't wait to spend time with you. He's so in love with you that He constantly sends little gifts to let you know He's thinking about you. He's God—and He simply loves to love you.

21

God loves when you see and hear Him.

"But blessed are your eyes because they see, and your ears because they hear."

—MATTHEW 13:16

What do you see? What do you hear? No, not with your physical eyes or ears. With your heart. When you open the eyes and ears of your heart to God, what do you see? What do you hear?

Him.

When you look and listen for God, you'll discover that He's always there. He sends you flowers in springtime and snowflakes in winter. You can hear His joy echo in a child's laugh and glimpse His love in a mother's gaze. He's with you always . . . and He loves when you see and hear Him.

22

God loves your ashes.

*He has sent me to bind up
the brokenhearted, . . .
to comfort all who mourn, . . .
to bestow on them a crown of beauty
instead of ashes.*

—ISAIAH 61:1–3

What does your crown look like? Is it chipped and dented by past mistakes? Is it fragile with the worried fumblings of what-ifs and what-might-have-beens? Is it covered with the ashes burned out by sorrows and broken dreams?

Take it off. Drop to your knees and give it to God. He'll take away your battered old crown and give you a new one. One that shines with His light, sparkles with His hope. A crown fit for a child of the King. Yes, God loves your ashes because He can fashion them into a beautiful crown.

23

God loves to hear you call Him "Father."

Let us then approach God's throne of grace with confidence, so that we may receive mercy and find grace to help us in our time of need.

—HEBREWS 4:16

Maybe your earthly father is wonderful, the best dad in the world. Or maybe he isn't. But no matter what he is like, you have a Father who loves you . . . *perfectly.*

No matter what you've got to say, He's waiting to listen. No matter what you need, He's waiting to provide. No matter what you've done, He's waiting to forgive. Don't be shy. Go to Him, climb into His lap, and rest your head on His shoulder. It's okay. Really. You're His child. And He loves to hear you call Him "Abba, Father, Dad."

24

God loves your kindness.

"Truly I tell you, whatever you did for one of the least of these brothers and sisters of mine, you did for me."

—MATTHEW 25:40

He noticed, you know. What you did, He saw. What you said, He heard.

You gave your lunch to that homeless guy, your time to that hurting friend. You stooped to lift up, you stood up for, you reached out a hand. You might not even remember it. It was just a little thing, a part of who you are because of *whose* you are.

But it wasn't little to the one you stooped for, stood up for, reached out to. And it wasn't little to Him because it was really *for* Him. A gift of kindness from you to Him.

25

God loves the way you light up a room.

"Let your light shine before others, that they may see your good deeds and glorify your Father in heaven."

—MATTHEW 5:16

People know when you mean it. When "How are you?" is more than a polite, passing question. When "Let me know how I can help" is more than an excuse to walk away. When your smile reaches your eyes and the words come from your heart, people know it. They know it by the light. It fills the room, chases away the shadows, and shines brighter than any star in the heavens. It's the light of God's love, and when you let it shine through your life—He loves *you* for it.

26

God loves your confidence.

Being confident of this, that he who began a good work in you will carry it on to completion until the day of Christ Jesus.

—PHILIPPIANS 1:6

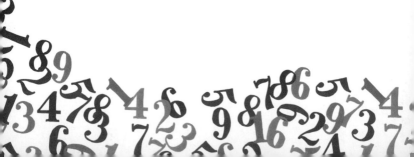

Okay . . . so maybe you don't always feel confident, but you can be. It's there for you, just waiting to be claimed. Not because of what you do, but because of what He did. Not because of who you are, but because of who He is. Not because of what you know or say, but because of who you know and what He promised.

You are His. You may not have it all figured out, but He does. And He won't stop working on you until you are made complete in Christ. You can be confident in that.

27

God loves your giving heart.

*"Give, and it will be given to you.
A good measure, pressed down,
shaken together and running
over, will be poured into your lap.
For with the measure you use,
it will be measured to you."*

—LUKE 6:38

It's often easy to give . . . a few dollars here, some old clothes there. Not so much that you really even notice. But when you dig down, when you stretch yourself and give like the widow with her two mites, that's when God really smiles.

It's offering the time you didn't have. The listening ear when you didn't really want to listen. The money set aside to treat yourself. When you give from the heart, God blesses you more richly than you could ever imagine. You simply can't out-give God . . . though He loves to see you try.

28

God loves the way you trust Him.

"I give them eternal life, and they shall never perish; no one will snatch them out of my hand."

—JOHN 10:28

Do you ever skip to the last page? Ever just have to know how it all ends? Did the butler really do it? Did the guy get the girl? But even when you know the end, you still don't know the middle—the hows, whens, and wheres.

Kind of like life, isn't it? You can know the end because God promises His children a happily ever after. But the middle is part of the mystery of life. Mystery calls for trust. And when you trust your life to God, no one can *ever* snatch you out of His hand.

29

God loves the real you.

"I have loved you with an everlasting love;
I have drawn you with unfailing kindness."

—JEREMIAH 31:3

No makeup. Hair all a mess. Sneakers and sweats. No polish, no poise, no primp. It's the real you, all natural and unadorned. The one loved by God. You see . . .

You don't have to put on a show for God; you just have to show up.

You don't have to have it all together; you just have to know the One who put it all together.

You don't have to wear designer clothes; you just have to be clothed in Him.

It's the ultimate come-as-you-are party. God created you—drew you—from the riches of His imagination and out of the wealth of His love and kindness. And He loves the way you are drawn.

30

God loves your "Good mornings."

In the morning, Lᴏʀᴅ, you hear my voice;
in the morning I lay my requests before you
and wait expectantly.

—PSALM 5:3

With a yawn and a stretch, your eyes peek over the edge of the blanket just as the morning sun peeps over the horizon. Maybe you're bright and eager and bouncing out of bed. Or maybe you're mumbly and grumbly and pulling the covers back over your head.

Either way, don't forget the very best way to start your day is by saying "Good morning!" to the One who made it. Because the One who tells the sun to rise just loves to hear your voice . . . first thing in the morning.

31

God loves the way you sing.

Because you are my help,
I sing in the shadow of your wings.

—PSALM 63:7

It doesn't matter if you sing like an angel or if you can't carry a tune in the proverbial bucket. When you sing God's praises, you're part of His heavenly choir—there's never a note out of tune.

And with God as your heavenly Director, you can sing through the shadows of life and dance through both sunshine and storms. Because no matter what the weather of your life is like, God loves to shelter you under His wings while you sing.

32

God loves when you do what Jesus did.

When Jesus landed and saw a large crowd, he had compassion on them, because they were like sheep without a shepherd.

—MARK 6:34

You smiled. You stopped to help. You offered. You touched. You noticed the people around you. Took a moment to see them—really see them—just the way He did and just the way He still does. And God loves you for it.

Why? Because Jesus smiled. He stopped to help. He offered. He touched. He noticed the people around Him and took a moment to really see them. And when you do the things that Jesus did, God loves you for it.

33

God loves to lift you up.

Lord my God, I called to you for help,
and you healed me.

—PSALM 30:2

The Devil thinks he's winning. It's been a terrible day—loss, failure, disasters big or small. Whatever happened has knocked you to your knees, and the Devil has got you beat . . . or so he thinks. Little does he know that on your knees is the place of your greatest hope and greatest strength. It's the place of prayer. The place where you reach up to God and the place where He reaches down to you, to help and to heal because God loves to lift you up.

34

God loves to answer your call.

I call out to the LORD,
and he answers me from his holy mountain.

—PSALM 3:4

There's never a busy signal. No endless, unanswered ringing. No voicemail. Not with God. When you call, God answers. *Every. Single. Time.* Who else can promise that? More importantly, who else can deliver that?

God promises that when you call out to Him, He will answer. It may not be the answer you expect—it may not even be the answer you had hoped for—but it will always be the answer that is best for you. You can count on it. And you can count on Him because He always takes your call.

35

God loves the way you delight in His creation.

*"You will go out in joy
and be led forth in peace;
the mountains and hills
will burst into song before you,
and all the trees of the field
will clap their hands."*

—ISAIAH 55:12

God longs to delight you, to fill you with the wonder of His creation. He wants be your greatest romance. The most charming of all princes. He woos you with butterflies in springtime and jewel-colored leaves in the fall. He paints the skies with sunsets every evening and sunrises every morning. He gifts you with soaring mountains and azure oceans and endless starry skies. And when you notice, He fills you with His joy, His peace, and His song. Because God loves to be your delight.

36

God loves the way you lean on Him.

God is our refuge and strength,
an ever-present help in trouble.

—PSALM 46:1

*E*ver-present. Think about that for a moment—how many things in your life are truly ever-present? Friendships may come and go. Jobs can change in an instant. Even family may move away or, worse, turn away.

But God is never transitory. He doesn't come and go. He never changes (Hebrews 13:8). And though you may sometimes turn from Him, He doesn't turn from you. He's always there, *ever-present*, waiting to be your refuge and your strength. So lean on Him—He loves it.

37

God loves the way you let Him rescue you.

Reach down your hand from on high;
deliver me and rescue me
from the mighty waters.

—PSALM 144:7

You're drowning. Going down for the third count. No, it's not water that's swallowing you; it's the world. Maybe it's a too-long to-do list in a too-short day. Or the slings and arrows of gossips who delight in your struggles. Or loneliness, weariness, or emptiness. Whatever the cause, you're drowning and you are at the mercy of threatening waves. But like Peter, you reach up to God and cry out, "Lord, save me!" (Matthew 14:30). And He does . . . because rescuing you is just something He loves to do.

38

God loves the new you.

Therefore, if anyone is in Christ, the new creation has come: The old has gone, the new is here!

—2 CORINTHIANS 5:17

You sparkle. You shine. You've just got that certain air about you. And it's irresistible . . . to God. No, it's not the new "do." It's not even those gorgeous new shoes. It's *you*—the *new* you, completely made over, re-created in Christ.

Yes, you'll still make mistakes sometimes. And no, you're not perfect. But you are *perfectly made new*. And God just loves the way it looks on you.

39

God loves to hear your praises.

Lord, you are my God;
I will exalt you and praise your name,
for in perfect faithfulness
you have done wonderful things,
things planned long ago.

—ISAIAH 25:1

Birdsong in spring. The gentle sound of falling rain. A child's innocent laughter. There are so many beautiful sounds in this world, but there is none more beautiful to God than the sound of your praises.

> LORD, you are my God . . . you have done wonderful things. (Isaiah 25:1)

> There is none like you . . . you alone are God. (Psalm 86:8, 10)

Sing His praises out loud. Whisper them softly. Repeat them over and over. They're His most favorite sounds in the world!

40

God loves your courage.

"Have I not commanded you? Be strong and courageous. Do not be afraid; do not be discouraged, for the Lord your God will be with you wherever you go."

—JOSHUA 1:9

Courage isn't always about swords; sometimes it's about . . . smiles.

It's finding a way to laugh through tears and to praise through pain. It's figuring out how to smile in the face of stormy trials and troubles. No, not because you enjoy the storm, but because you know the One who controls it, the One who will never leave you to weather it all alone. When storm clouds darken your horizon, be strong, smile, and remember: the One who loves you is right by your side.

41

God loves the way you get in the game.

Be strong in the Lord and in his mighty power. Put on the full armor of God, so that you can take your stand against the devil's schemes.

—EPHESIANS 6:10–11

Sometimes being a spectator is good. Watching sports. Watching television. Even a little people-watching now and then can be quite interesting! But there are other times when being a spectator is not such a good thing. Like when it comes to living and loving and giving your life to God.

You see, faith is *not* a spectator sport. There are too many blessings to experience and too many souls at stake. So suit up and take a stand! Buckle up that belt of truth, strap on the breastplate of righteousness, and pick up the sword of God's Word. Because God loves to see you get in the game.

42

God loves your tender heart.

"Love your neighbor as yourself."

—MATTHEW 22:39

Your heart bursts with joy, breaks with tears, and even thumps with outrage at injustice. You let the sorrows, the joys, the struggles of those around you touch your heart. It can be a heavy load to bear, but remember . . .

Jesus' heart burst with joy over the little children, broke at the loss of a friend, and was outraged by the thieves in His Father's house. He bore the burden of loving the people around Him . . . and He will help you bear it too. Because both He and His Father love your tender heart.

43

God loves
your eyes.

*Open my eyes that I may see
wonderful things in your law.*

—PSALM 119:18

Y ou have beautiful eyes. More than just the physical, visible beauty of their shape and color. Rather, it's the way you let Jesus color and shape what you see. It's the way His light and His love shine through. And it's the way you let Him show you how to truly see and how to truly serve.

Blessed are those who open their eyes to see the wonders of a life lived for the Lord—and blessed are your beautiful eyes.

44

God loves your tears.

Jesus wept.

—JOHN 11:35

Tears of joy. Tears of sorrow. Tears of frustration. There are days when the tears fall like raindrops for all the world to see. And there are times when you hide your tears away so that no one can see.

But God sees. *Always.* He knows every tear that falls, and He writes them in the records of heaven (Psalm 56:8). He holds your heart in His hands and your tears in His heart.

It's not that God loves to *see* you in sorrow or in pain. It's not that He loves to *see* your tears. But He loves the way your tears draw you nearer, still nearer, to Him.

45

God loves the way you flavor His world.

"You are the salt of the earth."

—MATTHEW 5:13

A dash of salt can make all the difference in the flavor of a dish. And so it is with a dash of faith. It can make all the difference in the flavor of a life.

A hope-filled note can brighten a hopeless day. A forgiving heart can lighten a heavy load of guilt. A kind word, a loving touch could be just the glimpse of Jesus that some lost soul needs.

Wherever you go, whatever you do, whatever words you speak, season them with a dash of faith—because God loves the way you flavor His world.

46

God loves your persistence.

"So I say to you: Ask and it will be given to you; seek and you will find; knock and the door will be opened to you."

—LUKE 11:9

When you don't know the answer, keep asking. When you're not sure which way to go, keep searching. When you simply don't know what to do, keep praying. Always, always, *always* keep praying.

Because God does listen. He does hear. And He does answer. In His own perfect time and in His own perfect way. Until then, keep knocking. God will open the door because He loves your persistence.

47

God loves the way you bloom.

"Consider how the wild flowers grow. They do not labor or spin. Yet I tell you, not even Solomon in all his splendor was dressed like one of these."

—LUKE 12:27

very flower starts with a seed, and every beautiful bloom begins in the dirt. So when your heart is hard from the difficulties of this world, when you're covered with the muck and mire of mistakes—that's not the time to give up. That's the time to give in, to surrender completely to God and His perfect plan.

Because He is the Master Gardener. Just look at the wildflowers—no king ever wore such splendor. Give God your hardened heart, with all its messines, and let Him help you bloom.

48

God loves the way you dig.

All Scripture is God-breathed and is useful for teaching, rebuking, correcting and training in righteousness, so that the servant of God may be thoroughly equipped for every good work.

—2 TIMOTHY 3:16–17

*D*ig. It brings to mind things like soil, seeds, and the tools with which to dig. Now imagine that God's Word is the soil and your heart is the seed. *Dig* down into His Word. Open up the Bible and drag out your tools: the dictionary, concordance, and commentaries. Drop to your knees, and plant yourself in Him. Pray and listen.

When you dig into God's Word, it enriches your life, guards your heart, and guides your actions. You don't have to be some great scholar —just dig in and God will bless you for it.

49

God loves the way you smile.

A happy heart makes the face cheerful, but heartache crushes the spirit.

—PROVERBS 15:13

A goofy grin or a shy little smile. Beaming from ear to ear. Whatever your style, your smile is one of your most beautiful features. Because it isn't really about lips or teeth or rosy cheeks. It's about being so full of the love and joy and hope and kindness of the Lord that you simply can't hold it in. You've just got to share it with the world . . . with a great big grin!

Yes, God loves the way you smile, especially when it's because of Him.

50

God loves the way you laugh.

Our mouths were filled with laughter,
our tongues with songs of joy. . . .
The LORD has done great things for us,
and we are filled with joy.

—PSALM 126:2–3

The stars declare the glory of God. The mountains proclaim His might. But some things . . . don't you know that some things were created simply to make you laugh? Why else would a giraffe have such a long, spotted neck? Why else would an elephant have a trunk on its front? And there's simply no other reason for that tuxedoed penguin waddle than to make you giggle and grin.

Some people actually say that laughter is not of God. Don't believe it! Let the world ring with your giggles, chuckles, and snorts—because God loves to hear your laughter.

51

God loves to watch you grow.

Jesus grew in wisdom and stature,
and in favor with God and man.

—LUKE 2:52

G od watched His Son as He grew from a baby in a manger to man on a mission. And when Jesus was baptized, He came down like a dove to say, "You are my Son, whom I love; with you I am well pleased" (Luke 3:22).

Just as God watched Jesus grow, He's watching you too. He's watching you grow in wisdom as you learn from His Word. He's watching you grow stronger as you trust Him to strengthen you. As you grow, your proud Papa, your Abba, says, *You are my child, whom I love; with you I am well pleased.*

52

God loves your hands.

The Lord your God will bless you in all your harvest and in all the work of your hands, and your joy will be complete.

—DEUTERONOMY 16:15

Holding, lifting, touching, serving. So many things your hands can do. For God, for others, and for you.

Palms lifted up in praise. Fingers wet with wiped-away tears or sticky with the messes of children, of life, of service. The work of your hands may not always seem important to you or to a world too busy to take notice. But to the one you touch, to the one whose tears you wipe away, and to the One your hands really serve, there are few gifts more precious. God loves the work of your hands.

53

God loves your feet.

*How beautiful on the mountains
are the feet of those who bring good news,
who proclaim peace,
who bring good tidings,
who proclaim salvation,
who say to Zion,
"Your God reigns!"*

—ISAIAH 52:7

Barefoot in the sand, splashing through the puddles, or tottering in high heels. Your feet carry you wherever you want to go. So let them carry you to worship. Let them carry you to friends in need. Let them carry you to those who don't know Him, to those who need both good news and the Good News. When your feet carry you closer to God and to those who need Him, He blesses every step you take

54

God loves His handiwork.

*For we are God's handiwork,
created in Christ Jesus to do
good works, which God prepared
in advance for us to do.*

—EPHESIANS 2:10

God created the sun to give His world heat and light. He created the rain to give it water. He filled it with fruits and foods to nourish and sustain. All the beauty and wonder and majesty of this world are His handiwork. But the creation He loves best? The creation He sent His Son to save? The creation He trusts to do the works of His will? *You.* Because when God wanted a creation to serve Him and to glorify His name . . . He created you. His wonderful, beautiful handiwork.

55

God loves the way you work.

Whatever you do, work at it with all your heart, as working for the Lord. . . . It is the Lord Christ you are serving.

—COLOSSIANS 3:23–24

eeding the hungry. Clothing the poor. Saving the lost in a faraway land. *Now that's serving the Lord!* you think. And it is. But most days aren't nearly that glamorous. Yet even on the most unglamorous, ordinary, mundane sort of day, you can glorify God in everything you do.

Everything? Yep, everything. *Vacuuming the floors?* Mmm-hmm. *Tackling that endless Everest of laundry?* Absolutely. *Even scrubbing the toilets!* Without a doubt.

Whether you're front and center in a starring role or behind the scenes and under the radar, when you work with a heart that loves the Lord, you glorify Him in everything you do.

56

God loves your words.

Like apples of gold in settings of silver is a ruling rightly given.

—PROVERBS 25:11

You chose the gift so carefully. *It's just what he needs. It's just what she's hoping for.* You wrapped it in the prettiest package you could find, topped it with a bow, and presented it with a smile. It made her day. It really was just what he needed. The perfect gift. It didn't come from a jewelry store; it came from your heart. Words gifted like apples of gold in a setting of silver. Words of encouragement, words of life that God loves to hear from your lips.

57

God loves your thirst for Him.

*"Whoever drinks the water
I give them will never thirst.
Indeed, the water I give them
will become in them a spring of
water welling up to eternal life."*

—JOHN 4:14

Parched. Dry. Aching. Not your throat, but your soul. It isn't water you need, but living water. And there's only one place to get it. From the living stream.

Run from this dry, barren desert of a world to the oasis of God's Word. Drink long and deep. Let Him quench your thirst, restore, and renew. Rest in the cool of His shadow. God loves your thirst because it sends you running to Him . . . because it lets Him refresh you from the living stream.

58

God loves the way you keep going.

*Trust in the LORD with all your heart
and lean not on your own understanding;
in all your ways submit to him,
and he will make your paths straight.*

—PROVERBS 3:5–6

Well . . . that last-minute change certainly wasn't part of your plan. And that crisis? It definitely wasn't on your calendar. What's a person to do? *Hang on. Hold on. Believe and trust.* God's got a plan, a good and perfect plan just for you. He can—and will—use this for your good. Somehow and some way. So take a deep breath, say a prayer, and take the next step. Because God loves the way you keep calm and trust on.

59

God loves the way you see.

"People look at the outward appearance, but the Lord looks at the heart."

—1 SAMUEL 16:7

When you give your heart to God, He changes the way you see yourself, the world, the people around you. You begin to see as God sees.

You see the sadness behind the smile, the pain instead of the scars, the loneliness behind the bitterness, and the desperation beneath the dirt.

And when you see—*truly see*—you can help. You can become the hands and feet of God. And you can lead the blind to the only One who can open their eyes. So . . . God loves the way you see.

60

God loves your humbleness.

Do nothing out of selfish ambition or vain conceit. Rather, in humility value others above yourselves, not looking to your own interests but each of you to the interests of the others.

—PHILIPPIANS 2:3–4

You're awesome. You're fabulous. You're simply amazing! After all, you're God's own creation. You sparkle with His Spirit and shine with His love. But your shine is never brighter than when you're helping others to discover their own sparkle and shine. It's when you say, *You take the lead, I know you can do it*, and *You would be so wonderful at that.*

When you consider others better than yourself, when you humble your heart, your ego, and your pride, you are truly a glittering jewel in God's heavenly crown.

61

God loves
your hope.

And I will hope in your name,
for your name is good.

—PSALM 52:9

Maybe it's been a rough day or week. Maybe even a rough month or year. It may even have been a rough life. But you keep going. You keep clinging to your Savior's hand. You keep *hoping*. Because you *know* what is promised, and because you *know* the One who promised is faithful. And because you *know* He loves you and your beautiful, shining hope.

62

God loves
your quirks.

*You have searched me, LORD,
and you know me.*

—PSALM 139:1

Can you balance a spoon on the end of your nose? Or hum the entire *William Tell Overture* from start to finish? Or maybe you know the entire play-by-play of baseball's famous "Who's on first?" act. Everyone has her own special talents, her own unique ways, her . . . quirks. They are all part of God's gifts to you—yes, even the quirkiest quirks— and they're just one more thing that He loves about you.

63

God loves your gifts.

Do not neglect your gift.

—1 TIMOTHY 4:14

Why can't I sing like her? Why can't I teach like him? Why can't I . . . It's so easy to look at the gifts of others and then see yourself as lacking. You can end up feeling frumpy, invisible, and of not much use. Because as surely as the sun rises, you too are a gifted creation of God—you just have to discover and open His gift. Not sure of your gift? Ask God to show you. Then open it up, put it to use, and watch as God uses you to His great glory—because God created you to be a gift.

64

God loves your fruitful life.

But the fruit of the Spirit is love, joy, peace, forbearance, kindness, goodness, faithfulness, gentleness and self-control. Against such things there is no law.

—GALATIANS 5:22–23

When you plant yourself in God, you begin to grow like a tree planted by streams of water. And as you grow, your life begins to yield fruit. Not fruit for the body, but fruit for soul.

You bloom with love and joy. Peace pervades your presence. Patience, kindness, and goodness become the ways of your life. Faithfulness and self-control sustain you. And when your life is filled with fruit, its abundance spills out to nourish those around you—and God loves your fruitful, fruit-filled life.

65

God loves the way you love Him.

"Love the Lord your God with all your heart and with all your soul and with all your mind and with all your strength."

—MARK 12:30

Loving God should be all-in, full-out, no-holds-barred. Like diving into the pool on that first hot day of summer. Cool and refreshing.

So don't just dip your toe in the water. There's no need to wade in slowly. This is the time for a cannonball! Let Him splash out all over your life and everyone around you. God wants you to jump into the deep end of His love, to love Him with everything you've got. Heart, soul, mind, and strength. Why? 'Cause that's the way He loves you . . . *all-in, full-out, no-holds-barred!*

66

God loves your dreams.

"For I know the plans I have for you," declares the Lord, "plans to prosper you and not to harm you, plans to give you hope and a future."

—JEREMIAH 29:11

What do you dream about? Someone to love and to be loved by? A fabulous and successful career? A life filled with purpose and meaning? Whatever your dream, God has a bigger one, a better one. A dream dreamed just for you, and a plan to make it all come true. God's dream for your life might look a lot like yours, or it might look completely different.

When you give your life to God, He takes your dreams and shapes them into something bigger, something better, something . . . *eternal*. He makes your dreams one with His own. And then He makes them come true.

67

God loves your friendship.

"Love each other as I have loved you. Greater love has no one than this: to lay down one's life for one's friends. You are my friends if you do what I command."

—JOHN 15:12–14

What does *friendship* mean to you? Is it someone who always listens, is always on your side? Someone who always lifts up and encourages? Maybe it's someone who loves you enough say, "You're wrong," yet who also cares enough to help you make it right. A true friend is that person who knows everything about you—your weaknesses, your flaws, your fears, and your shame—and still does not go away. You have a friend like that, you know. A best friend.

You know Him. You know His name. He's the One who loves you so much that He laid down His life for you, His friend. *Follow Him.* Be His friend as He is yours.

68

God loves the child in you.

Jesus called the children to him and said, "Let the little children come to me, and do not hinder them, for the kingdom of God belongs to such as these."

—LUKE 18:16

ainbows still stop you in your tracks. Splashing through mud puddles is your secret delight. And, let's be honest, there are few things more wonderful than a chocolate chip cookie dunked into ice-cold milk. No matter your age, there's always that part of you that never quite completely grows up. The part that giggles at knock-knock jokes and is still amazed by the endless, everyday miracles of life.

It's okay, you know. There's no need to completely grow up. Jesus is delighted by little children, and He's delighted by the child in you. So go ahead . . . dunk that cookie . . . and, yeah, lick the spoon too.

69

God loves
your scars.

*The LORD is close to the brokenhearted
and saves those who are crushed in spirit.*

—PSALM 34:18

cars. Everyone has them. Some are visible, others invisible, but no less deeply felt. Some are scars of the skin; others are scars of the heart. There are those who will take your scars and use them as a reason not to love you, not to be your friend. They can make you feel *less than, damaged, broken, unworthy.* But not God.

God sees your scars, even the invisible ones. But He uses them as a reason to lavish you with His healing love. He uses your brokenness to draw you close to Him and to make you whole.

70

God loves when you bring Him your mangled messes.

But the pot he was shaping from the clay was marred in his hands; so the potter formed it into another pot, shaping it as seemed best to him.

—JEREMIAH 18:4

Well . . . you grew tired of waiting on God and took things into your own hands. And you messed up. *Royally.* And that thing—that relationship, that project, that piece of your life that you were trying so desperately to make "just so"—is now a mangled mess. And it's your own fault, really. *What good am I to God now?* you wonder.

Give the mangled mess, the marred lump of clay that is your life, to God, the Master Potter. He will mold and shape you into a new creation—beautiful and precious, useful and good to Him.

71

God loves your imagination.

Now to him who is able to do immeasurably more than all we ask or imagine, according to his power that is at work within us.

—EPHESIANS 3:20

You can imagine a better world, a better life, a better way. But standing between imagination and reality are all the problems, challenges, and obstacles of this world. And you think, *I can only do so much!*

And that's true. On your own, *you* can only do so much. Which is actually great news— because you aren't on your own! Yahweh, the Lord God of all creation, is with you, and He can do so much more than you could ever imagine—*immeasurably more.* Unexpected solutions, inspired answers, untapped resources. So go ahead . . . ask God, and let Him give you a glimpse of *His* imagination.

72

God loves your joy.

The LORD is my strength and my shield;
my heart trusts in him, and he helps me.
My heart leaps for joy,
and with my song I praise him.

—PSALM 28:7

*J*oy. It's much more than laughter and good times, much more than simple happiness. True and everlasting joy is trusting when you don't understand, believing the unbelievable, and hoping in the face of hopelessness.

True joy is stepping out in faith, off the proverbial cliff, and knowing that the One who holds up the heavens will hold you up no matter what the circumstances may be. Because He loves you, loves your trust, and loves your faith. Because He loves your joy.

73

God loves your goodness.

"But a Samaritan, as he traveled, came where the man was; and when he saw him, he took pity on him. He went to him and bandaged his wounds, pouring on oil and wine. Then he put the man on his own donkey, brought him to an inn and took care of him."

—LUKE 10:33–34

You really didn't have to do that. You didn't have to go out of your way. Didn't have to get involved or get your hands dirty. But you did. You went the extra mile. Not to be seen. Not for any reward. But simply because it was the right thing—the *good* thing—to do.

And you know all about goodness. After all, you learned it from the Master Himself. Because He is so good to you, and because you want to be like Him, your goodness is just one more thing for Him to love about you.

74

God loves your creativity.

*"It is I who made the earth
and created mankind on it.
My own hands stretched out the heavens;
I marshaled their starry hosts."*

—ISAIAH 45:12

Feeling creative? How about inventive? Or daring? Because that's who God made you to be. You are made in the image of Elohim, the Creator God, the One who paints the mornings, invented oceans, and sculpted mountains. His creativity, His inventiveness, and His daring are part of you.

Don't be afraid to think outside the box. Show your creative flair. Dare to dream. The creativity of God lives inside of you. Let it out. Make the world your canvas, for God loves the uniquely creative touch that only you can add to His world.

75

God loves the way you rest in Him.

He who watches over you will not slumber.

—PSALM 121:3

It's been a long day. The world has thrown its best—and its worst—at you. By the grace of God, you're still standing. But you're tired, so very tired. The tank is empty, and you're running on fumes.

Slip away. Find a quiet place—even if it's only in your mind. For a moment, for an hour, for a day. Lay down those heavy burdens. Rest your weary head on the shoulder of the One who never sleeps, who never tires, who never ceases to watch over you because He loves you, and He loves to hold you while you rest your weary soul in Him.

76

God loves the way you run.

Let us run with perseverance the race marked out for us, fixing our eyes on Jesus, the pioneer and perfecter of faith.

—HEBREWS 12:1–2

You run. Sometimes strong and sure, sometimes haltingly, stumbling now and then. But never stopping. One foot in front of the other, following the path laid out before you—even when you're not sure what's around the next turn. Your goal isn't to finish first, but simply to finish. Building stamina and strength, confidence and faith.

As you run, you encourage others to join the race. You cheer on your fellow athletes, lifting up those who have fallen. And when you yourself grow weary, you lean on the One who runs right by your side. Because He doesn't want to miss a moment. Because He loves to see you run.

77

God loves the way you forget.

But one thing I do: Forgetting what is behind and straining toward what is ahead, I press on toward the goal to win the prize for which God has called me heavenward in Christ Jesus.

—PHILIPPIANS 3:13–14

Past mistakes, lost opportunities, regrets, and closed doors—the evil one likes to remind you of these things. Whispering poison in your ear, he tries to hold you back, make you stumble as you remember.

But you *choose* to forget. And for those things that you cannot forget, you *choose* not to remember. Because no matter what shadows darken your past, you've given yourself to the One who washes you clean and guarantees your future. And the only One who truly matters loves the way you forget the past and look instead toward the heavenly goal.

78

God loves your choices.

*"Choose for yourselves this
day whom you will serve. . . .
As for me and my household,
we will serve the Lord."*

—JOSHUA 24:15

Life is all about choices, but eternal life is all about choosing God and choosing *His* way.

- You could choose to be angry, but you choose to forgive.
- You could choose to be idle, but you choose to serve.
- You could choose to be selfish and self-indulgent, but you choose self-sacrifice.
- You could choose to get even, but you choose to let go.
- You could choose to simply walk away, but you choose to stay.
- You could choose jealousy and bitterness, but you choose joy.
- You could choose the world, but you choose God . . . and He loves your choice.

79

God loves your need.

And my God will meet all your needs according to the riches of his glory in Christ Jesus.

—PHILIPPIANS 4:19

ood, clothing, shelter. All the basic needs of life, right? Oh, and maybe chocolate.

God knows all that you need and He promises to provide all that you need. But you have one need that is greater than any other—the need for Someone to do for you what you can never do for yourself. You need Someone to wash away every mistake, every bad decision, every willful wrong choice. You need Someone to save you—so God sent a Savior

The day you realize that He is your greatest need is the day you go running to Him—which is why God loves your need.

80

God loves your heavenly treasures.

"Store up for yourselves treasures in heaven, where moths and vermin do not destroy, and where thieves do not break in and steal. For where your treasure is, there your heart will be also."

—MATTHEW 6:20–21

It doesn't matter whether your bank account is big or small. Or if your rainy-day fund has seen more storm clouds than sun. Or whether your jewels came from Tiffany's or were a flea market find. None of these things matter. Not to God.

A day will come will come when all the money, all the diamonds and jewels, all the riches of this world will pass away. And only the true treasures will remain. Things like kindness, generosity, faithfulness, and joy. These are the treasures to invest in. These are the treasures that last, tucked away in heaven for you by the Lord who loves you.

81

God loves when you open the door.

"Here I am! I stand at the door and knock. If anyone hears my voice and opens the door, I will come in and eat with that person, and they with me."

—REVELATION 3:20

He stands. He knocks. He waits. But opening the door? That's up to you. Because He will never push it open or break it down. He will never threaten or shout. He will simply knock and wait for you to answer, for you to invite Him in.

And when you do choose to open that door, the angels in heaven rejoice and your Savior smiles! For one of God's greatest joys is when you open the door.

82

God loves the way you remember.

Give praise to the LORD . . .
Remember the wonders he has done.

—PSALM 105:1, 5

You know God is at work in your life. You know it as surely as you breathe. You've seen it with your own eyes and you *remember* all the wonderful, marvelous, miraculous, incredible, and even outrageous things He has done for you. And because you remember, you count on Him, you thank Him, you serve Him, and you praise Him every day. Oh yes . . . God loves the way you *remember.*

83

God loves that you are a stranger in this world.

They were foreigners and strangers on earth. . . . They were longing for a better country—a heavenly one.

—HEBREWS 11:13, 16

So you don't quite fit in. You're that square peg stuck in a round hole. And, at times, you stick out like a sore thumb. Good. Yes . . . *good!* That's what God loves to see.

Because those who conform to the ways of this world—those who blend in, who go along simply to get along—belong to the Prince who rules this world. But not you; *you* are just passing through. So don't be afraid to stand out. Be glad you're a stranger in this world—because God certainly is!

84

God loves your faithfulness.

The Lord rewards everyone for their righteousness and faithfulness.

—1 SAMUEL 26:23

G od knows there are times when you don't understand His ways, but He sees you continue to follow Him. He knows there are times when His choices for you make you sad or even angry, but He sees you keep on choosing Him. He knows there are times when you just feel too exhausted to carry on, but He sees you lean into Him and let Him carry you.

Faithfulness, even when you're confused, hurt, and exhausted—that's what God sees. That's what God loves . . . because God is forever faithful to you.

85

God loves to watch your climb.

The Sovereign LORD is my strength;
he makes my feet like the feet of a deer,
he enables me to tread on the heights.

—HABAKKUK 3:19

You're a mountain climber . . . did you know that? Climbing up the mountains of this world, toward the top, toward the heavenly realms.

Some days are ever onward and upward, while others find you slipping and sliding. There are giant leaps of faith. And there are tiny, agonizing steps of blind trust, when your fingers cling to the cliff. But you anchor yourself in the solid rock of His Word, your arms fill with the strength of His Spirit, and you climb. Ever closer. Ever nearer to the One who reaches down to pull you up to the top, to the peak, to His side.

86

God loves the way you think.

Whatever is true, whatever is noble, whatever is right, whatever is pure, whatever is lovely, whatever is admirable—if anything is excellent or praiseworthy— think about such things.

—PHILIPPIANS 4:8

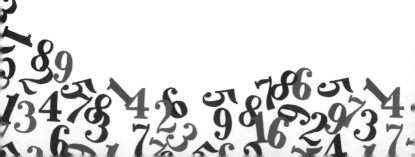

Turn on the television. Scan the movie ads. Pick up a newspaper. What do you see? The Devil doing his best to steal, kill, and destroy and to fill your mind with thoughts of malice, jealousy, anger, and just plain old evil.

But you stop the roaring lion in his tracks. How? By changing the channel. By seeking out movies that echo God's love. By turning to the back of the newspaper to find the buried stories of hope and courage. So while the Devil may try to hijack your thoughts with the filth of the world, you choose to think differently. You choose to think of God—and He *loves* the way you think.

87

God loves your obedience.

*"If you love me, keep
my commands."*

—JOHN 14:15

For the world, *obedience* is a four-letter word. Following Jesus is just about following rules. And faith is really another name for *thou shalt* and *thou shalt not*. At least, that's what the world sees.

But not you. You see obeying Jesus in a different light. Instead of seeing only what Jesus *asks* of you, you see the amazing, awesome, glorious picture of what He *gives* to you. Mercy! Grace! Salvation! And you know that His commands—which truly ask so very little of you—are to *protect* and to *save* you. Because He *loves* you.

88

God loves the way you listen.

"My sheep listen to my voice;
I know them, and they follow me."

—JOHN 10:27

*L*isten . . . did you hear that? Not the roar, not the rush, not the bullying shouts and screams of the world. But that? That still, small voice? That's *Him*—it really is. The Lord God of all, Yahweh, Elohim, Jehovah-jireh is speaking to you. Yes, *you*.

And because you are His, you know His voice. So you stop. You drop to your knees, even if it's only in your heart, and you listen. "Be still," He says, "and know that I am God" (Psalm 46:10). He loves the way you listen.

89

God loves the way you pray.

Pray continually.

—1 THESSALONIANS 5:17

Continually, constantly, unceasing, never stopping, over and over again.

In the car, in the shower, in the quiet of morning, in the still of the night, in the hustle and bustle of everyday life.

Eyes wide open, eyes tightly shut, head in your hands, on your knees, in your heart.

It's how you pray. And His answer? His answer is . . . incomprehensible peace, unfailing love, undeserved mercy, unearned grace, unmerited salvation. Oh yes . . . God loves the way you pray.

90

God loves the touch of your faith.

Jesus turned and saw her.
"Take heart, daughter," he said,
"your faith has healed you."

—MATTHEW 9:22

How frightened she must have been. Alone, untouchable, and untouched for so very long. And there He was, standing before her, her one last hope. Would she dare? *Perhaps just the hem of His robe.*

Tentative and trembling, she stretched out a hand. And Jesus felt, turned, and saw. He saw the heart that no one bothered to look at for so very long. He felt her touch of faith, and He gave her a new life.

No matter how tentative, how trembling your touch, Jesus feels it. He turns, He sees, He gives you a new life. Because He treasures the touch of your faith.

91

God loves the way you don't see.

For there is no difference between Jew and Gentile—the same Lord is Lord of all and richly blesses all who call on him.

—ROMANS 10:12

S ome people see only the differences. *She is so fat! Did you see his clothes? What is she doing on this side of town?* Shade of skin, heritage, size, weight, and age—instead of seeing these as amazing reminders of the creativity of God, some people see these differences as a reason to mock, to scorn, even to hate.

But you know that the God who loves, cherishes, and saves you is the same God who loves, cherishes, and longs to save everyone. Instead of differences, you see souls who need Jesus. And God loves the way you see *them* instead of their differences.

92

God loves the way you let Him lead.

"Come, follow me," Jesus said.

—MATTHEW 4:19

Living a faithful life is a lot like a dance—not a solo performance, mind you, but a grand waltz with twists and turns, dips and sways, intricate steps and tricky combinations. And as with any great dance, there must be a Leader and one who is led.

If you try to take the lead yourself, to spin off in your own direction, you'll end up in a tangled mess on the floor. You know that because you've been down there before. So you place your hand in His. You let His touch be your guide. And you trust Him to lead you safely through this dance of a faithful life.

93

God loves the way you fight.

*The LORD is my light and my salvation—
whom shall I fear? The LORD
is the stronghold of my life—
of whom shall I be afraid?*

—PSALM 27:1

Wait! What? God loves the way you *fight*? Yes!

There is war going on out there. A war for your soul, for your family, for your friends, for the stranger on the street. It's a war to silence you, to make you invisible, to deny the power of God. But you're not having it. You've suited up for battle, and you're ready to fight. Not with fists, but with a heavenly arsenal of truth, righteousness, peace, faith, salvation, and the living Word of God.

Underneath those heels and pearls, you are a sword-wielding, shield-carrying, armor-wearing warrior of God—and He loves the way you fight!

94

God loves your nearness.

Come near to God and he will come near to you.

—JAMES 4:8

Just a step. That's all it takes. Reach up to God, and He reaches down to you. Heavenly fingers grasp your hand, pull you close, and cradle your heart in His.

No matter how far you've wandered, no matter the mistakes you've made, He's waiting. Whether it's early in the morning, at the end of the day, or anytime in between, He's waiting. God waits for you, hoping you will come and ready when you do. Ready to wash away, to cleanse, to make new. Draw near to God because He loves to be near you.

95

God loves the way you shout His name!

*My lips will shout for joy
when I sing praise to you—
I whom you have delivered.*

—PSALM 71:23

The world around you whispers, *"Shhh!"* *Faith is a private thing*, they say. *You should keep it to yourself.* But it's too good! The news is too wonderful. You can't be quiet. You *won't* be quiet. Silence is for those who don't know your God; it's not for you.

"Come and see what God has done!" (Psalm 66:5). You shout out the greatness of God with your lips; you shout it out by the things you do; you shout it out through your whole life. The Lord God has delivered you and God loves the way you shout about it!

96

God loves your surrender.

"Father, if you are willing, take this cup from me; yet not my will, but yours be done."

—LUKE 22:42

Not my will, Lord, but Yours be done. Those aren't easy words to say, whether you've said them once or whether you've said them a million times. Laying down your will, surrendering all to Him isn't easy.

But you know there is nothing better. Because in your life you've discovered that your own foolish pride, your own willful stubbornness, your own best-laid plans are never as good as God's. So you surrender, you lay down your will at His feet. *Search me, God. You know my heart. Show me the wrongs I have done. Teach me. Lead me. I give my life to You. I surrender all.*

97

God loves your questions.

"For my thoughts are not your thoughts,
neither are your ways my ways,"
declares the LORD.

—ISAIAH 55:8

Why? How? When? The questions of life. Questions you cannot answer. Questions only God knows the answers to. But do you dare to ask?

Yes. Because God is big enough, powerful enough, all-knowing enough, and loves you enough to listen to your questions. And to answer. In His own perfect time. In His own perfect way. With His own perfect answer.

Through your questions and through His answers, God teaches you to trust. So yes, God loves your questions because they help you to better know Him.

98

God loves the way you seek.

"You will seek me and find me when you seek me with all your heart."

—JEREMIAH 29:13

In life, there are no guarantees. But with God, there are *only* guarantees. He keeps every promise. Every. Single. One. *Guaranteed.*

God doesn't mess around with some playground version of hide-and-seek. He *wants* you to find Him. And it's so easy to do. Just open His Word and He's there, waiting for you. Drop to your knees, open your heart in prayer, and He slips down from heaven to meet you. Seek Him with all your heart, and you *will* find Him. It's a promise that God makes with all of His heart. God loves your seeking because He loves to be found.

99

God loves your welcoming ways.

*Do not forget to show hospitality
to strangers, for by so doing some
people have shown hospitality
to angels without knowing it.*

—HEBREWS 13:2

They're everywhere, all around you. The lonely, the uncertain, the lost.

They're those scared, searching souls trying to slip onto the back pew and then slip back out again. They're the unlovely, the unlovable, and the unloved. They're the corner cashier, the stranger on the street, and the new kid in town.

And you welcome them. A smile, a hug, a handshake. You draw them into the circle of your friendship and introduce them to the love of God. To the One who loves your welcoming ways.

100

God loves . . . you.

*I praise you because I am fearfully
and wonderfully made;
your works are wonderful,
I know that full well.*

—PSALM 139:14

God loves you simply because you are . . . well . . . *you*.

He loves your imperfections, your quirkiness, your creativity. He loves that you are courageous, confident, kind. He loves the way you laugh, the way you work, the way you give. And He loves that you trust Him enough to call Him *Lord*, *Abba*, *Father*, and even *Friend*.

God loves you so much, *so very much*, that He sacrificed His own Son to save you. Because you are fearfully and wonderfully made . . . because you are *you* . . . because you are *His*.

More Things God Loves About Me

_____

_____

_____

_____

_____

_____

_____

_____

_____

_____

_____

_____

_____

_____

_____

_____

More Things God Loves About Me

_____

_____

_____

_____

_____

_____

_____

_____

_____

_____

_____

_____

_____

_____

_____

_____